WHAT IS INSOMNIA?

INSOMNIA SECRET BURSTED IN FEW PAGES, FROM OVERVIEW TO COGNITIVE BEHAVIOURAL THERAPY (CBT)

BY

Dr. Henry Scott

....*Dr Henry Scott*

© 2024 **Dr. Henry Scott**

All rights reserved, NO content of this book may be copied, duplicated, or transferred either for commercial purpose or personal use without the author's express written consent.

Author's Note

insomnia is a curable illness, Although its widespread, .
Understanding insomnia better will help you make better use of the
resources available to you for improving your quality of sleep.
This could entail engaging in CBT-I, maintaining appropriate sleep
hygiene, or discussing prescription drugs with a physician.
Symptoms of insomnia can also interfere with your waking hours,
such as irritation and daytime tiredness. Over time, a number of
medical disorders that can also make it difficult for you to fall
asleep may be exacerbated by insomnia.
But you can better comprehend your sleep cycles by becoming
more informed about the facts. It might also provide you with the
means to manage the illness and improve your quality of sleep.
I once experienced insomia, but I was able to overcome it!

YES, YOU CAN ALSO.

Table of content

Contents

Frequently asked questions about insomnia

How can I fix insomnia?
For insomnia, there are numerous approaches and remedies available. This may entail taking medications, CBT, and better sleeping habits all at once.

Will insomnia ever go away?
The underlying reason and intensity of insomnia will determine how long a person has trouble sleeping. Acute insomnia should go away in a few weeks with the help of lifestyle changes. However, it might be necessary to seek medical assistance if a person has trouble sleeping for longer than three months.

How long does insomnia last?
Insomnia lasting less than three months is referred to as short-term insomnia. More than three months are spent with chronic sleeplessness.

What is the quality of life like for an insomniac?
In addition to making it difficult to fall asleep, insomnia can make a person feel agitated, depressed, tired, and headachey. It might also make it harder to focus and raise the possibility of an accident. The functioning of the

heart, brain, and other bodily organs can also be impacted by chronic insomnia.

To what extent is insomnia common?
Insomnia in both its acute and chronic forms is extremely frequent. Approximately 10% of adults globally fit the criteria for insomnia disorder, while one in three adults experience symptoms of insomnia.

What does the term "an insomniac" mean?
The most frequent complaint about sleep is insomnia. An insomniac finds it difficult to go asleep or stay asleep. They might routinely get up too early. Lack of sleep can cause a variety of problems, including daytime drowsiness and fatigue, mood swings, anger, and anxiety, as well as an overall sense of being mentally and physically ill.

Is there a cure for insomnia and how is it treated?
Insomnia can be treated in a variety of ways, from minor lifestyle and habit adjustments to prescription drugs.

INTRODUCTION

Other names for insomnia include sleep disorders, sleep problems, and difficulty falling asleep. One common sleep issue that can make it difficult to fall or remain asleep is sleep hygiene. It may also result in excessive waking and difficulty falling back asleep. When you wake up, you could still feel exhausted. Your attitude and energy levels can be negatively impacted by insomnia. It may also have an impact on your quality of life, career, and health.

People often take sleep for granted until they start to experience sleep deprivation. Your ability to sleep is essential to your health. Your general health might be adversely affected, both significantly and somewhat, by poor sleep quality.

It's a good idea to discuss your sleep issues with your healthcare physician. They can frequently direct you to a resource or expert who can help you, or they can help you enhance your quality of sleep. In this manner, you can put sleep-related worries to rest and wake up feeling rejuvenated and prepared.

Everyone Might Experience Random Insomnia

Almost everyone experiences occasional insomnia. Insomnia is more likely to strike, though, if:

You are a female. Hormonal changes that occur during the menstrual cycle and menopause might be involved. Hot flashes and nocturnal sweats during menopause frequently interfere with sleep. Pregnancy is another usual time for insomnia.

You're over 60. Your chances of developing insomnia increase with age due to alterations in health and sleep patterns.

You suffer from a physical or mental health issue. A lot of problems that impact your physical or mental well-being can interfere with your sleep.

You're under a lot of stress. Short-term sleeplessness can be brought on by stress. Prolonged or severe stress can cause persistent sleeplessness.

You don't follow a set routine. Your sleep-wake cycle may be disturbed by things like traveling or switching shifts at work.

Sleep And Insomnia

What is insomnia?

Not getting the recommended amount of sleep is called insomnia. That may indicate inadequate sleep, poor quality sleep, or difficulty falling or staying asleep. Insomnia is a minor inconvenience for certain individuals. For some people, insomnia can cause serious problems. The causes of insomnia might also differ greatly.

10% of people worldwide suffer from insomnia, which is a recognized medical disorder. It can be treated in a variety of methods, such as with drugs and mental health services, and is typically not harmful.
The effects may intensify and worsen over time. When insomnia is severe or persistent, some of the symptoms become harmful.

SLEEP

There are numerous reasons why your body requires sleep, and science is currently working to fully comprehend these reasons. Experts are aware that getting too little sleep can result in sleep deprivation, which is typically uncomfortable and impairs optimal functioning. Depending on their age, adults typically require 7 to 9 hours of sleep every 24 hours. Getting enough sleep is essential for preserving both physical and mental well-being. On the other hand, insomnia is a prevalent sleep ailment that has the potential to cause sleep disturbances. Each has a different threshold for sleep duration.

How much sleep is needed?
Everyone requires a different quantity of sleep.

Adults require 7 to 9 hours, whereas

children require 9 to 13 hours on average.

Infants and toddlers require 12 to 17 hours.

If you're always exhausted during the day, you probably don't get enough sleep.

Different sleeping habits and what that means for you

Individual differences can be seen in the demands and habits related to sleep. Experts classify a wide range of sleep-related traits as "normal" due to these differences. Here are a few examples of this:

Early birds/early risers: Individuals who naturally prefer to go to bed and wake up early are known as early birds or early risers.

Night owls/late risers: Some people have a preference for staying up late.

Short sleepers: Some individuals have a lower innate need for sleep than others. Studies suggest that there might even be a hereditary explanation for that.

Learned sleep differences: Certain people form sleep habits for particular reasons, like their line of work.

Combat-experienced military personnel frequently develop light sleep habits due to the rigors and risks associated with their line of work. On the other end of the spectrum, some individuals develop a highly heavy sleep pattern in order to cope with ambient noise.

Natural shifts in the amount of sleep required:
Throughout your life, your sleep needs will fluctuate. Adults (age 18 and older) require between seven to nine hours of sleep every day, whereas infants require much more—between fourteen and seventeen hours.

Furthermore, sleeplessness may contribute to the development of the following:

- Anxiety
- Obesity
- Accidents
- Injuries
- Diabetes
- Hypertension
- Stroke
- Heart conditions
- Depression
- It can also impair one's performance at work and school and make it harder for them to carry out daily tasks

Check whether you suffer from insomnia

You have insomnia if you frequently:

❖ Find it difficult to fall asleep

❖ Wake up frequently during the night

❖ lie awake at night

❖ Wake up early and are unable to fall back asleep

❖ Feel tired even after waking up

❖ Find it difficult to nap during the day

❖ Feel irritable and tired during the day

❖ Find it difficult to focus during the day because you are tired

Short-term insomnia is the term used to describe insomnia that lasts for less than three months.
Long-term insomnia is defined as insomnia that persists for three months or more.

Insomnia and Aging

As people age, insomnia becomes more prevalent. As you age, you might:

Modify your sleeping habits. As you get older, sleep tends to become less restful, making noise or other disturbances in your environment more likely to wake you up. Your internal clock tends to advance with age, so as you get older, you may experience fatigue sooner in the evening and wake up earlier. However, the amount of sleep that older individuals require is usually the same as that of younger ones.

Adjust the level of your activity. You might engage in less social or physical activity. An inactive lifestyle might cause sleep disturbances. You may also be more prone to take a daily sleep if you lead a less active lifestyle. Nighttime napping might cause sleep disturbances.

Experience changes in your health. Depression, anxiety, and chronic discomfort from back issues or arthritis can all interfere with sleep. Sleep disturbances can result from conditions like prostate or bladder issues, which increase the likelihood that you'll need to urinate during the night. As people age, sleep apnea and restless legs syndrome become increasingly prevalent.

Increase your medication intake. Prescription drug use is generally higher among older adults than among younger adults. This increases the likelihood of medication-related sleeplessness.

Insomnia in Children and Teenagers

Teenagers and young children may also have sleep issues. However, some kids and teenagers just struggle with adhering to a regular bedtime or falling asleep due to a more delayed internal clock. Their preference is to sleep in later and go to bed later.

Insomnia in children can occur for similar reasons as in adults. These explanations could consist of:
- Stress medications
- Excessive use of caffeine
- Issues relating to one's physical or mental health
- Your child may develop insomnia if they regularly wake up too early or have difficulty falling or staying asleep.

Symptoms of insomnia in children often include:

- Daytime sleepiness or restlessness.
- Agitation and mood swings
- Recurring disciplinary problems
- Issues with concentration and memory

Usually, the first step in treating children's insomnia is

To set and maintain a strict bedtime.

Developing a relaxing nighttime routine and adhering to healthy sleep hygiene guidelines, such as limiting screen time before bed, are further beneficial suggestions.

Lowering your child's exposure to stress
Further advice on managing childhood insomnia might be obtained from a pediatrician or therapist.

Insomnia in Adulthood

Research from 2019 indicates that up to 75% of older persons suffer from some form of sleeplessness.
A few distinct variables, some of which may have a domino effect, are responsible for insomnia in older adults:

- Sleeping and staying asleep may be more difficult as you age because of changes in the circadian rhythms that control your sleep-wake cycle.

- Being retired can mean that you don't have a regular social calendar or a set schedule during the day, which can both exacerbate insomnia.

- Social isolation can contribute to loneliness and increase your chances of experiencing depression, which can also raise your risk of sleep problems.

- Age-related health issues, such as chronic pain syndromes, might also interfere with your sleep.

- If you're not getting enough sleep at night, you may experience daytime weariness and drowsiness. This may make you more likely to take a nap. Of course, napping can make you feel less exhausted at night, which can prolong a pattern of insomnia.

Insomnia and Depression

Research signifies a close connection between depression and insomnia:

Poor sleep seemed to dramatically increase the likelihood of depression, especially during stressful times, according to a 2016 meta-analysis of 34 research (Trusted Source).

In a 2018 studyTrusted Source, the risk of depression rose with the severity of persistent insomnia symptoms over time. The study included 1,126 persons without a diagnosis of depression or insomnia at the start of the study.

Moreover, insomnia and other sleeping problems are among the primary signs of depression.
Here's the good news, though: Whichever disease manifests first—insomnia or depression—the same medications frequently address both.

The most popular forms of treatment include:
CBT
Therapy
Antidepressants
Lifestyle modifications like frequent exercise, meditation, and better sleeping patterns.

Insomnia and pregnancy

Pregnancy-related insomnia is common, particularly in the first and third trimesters.
Many factors can cause you to have difficulty falling asleep, such as hormonal fluctuations, nausea, and an increased urge to urinate.

Pain, like cramping and back stiffness, as well as increased worry and concern about the growing obligations you'll encounter as a new parent

The good news is that insomnia connected to pregnancy normally fades and has no effect on the development of your unborn child. Nevertheless, getting the recommended amount of sleep is critical to your general health.

Making the following lifestyle adjustments could assist with pregnancy insomnia:

- Exercising frequently
- Eating a balanced diet
- Drinking plenty of water
- Adhering to a regular sleep pattern.
- Practicing relaxation methods over the day to support calm and reduce anxiety

- Having a warm bath prior to sleeping

To ensure they are safe to use while pregnant, ask your healthcare team before beginning any new workout regimens, prescription drugs, or dietary supplements.

Insomnia and anxiety

Have you ever stayed up late worrying about something you were unable to control?

Anxiety and insomnia are frequently linked, and the relationship can work both ways.

For starters, you may have trouble falling asleep if you are unable to ease lingering anxiety and panic. However, long-term insomnia might make you worry about how much sleep you're missing and make it harder to control uncomfortable and challenging emotions during the day.

A mental health professional's support can assist you in starting to address all of your symptoms, regardless of whether you're suffering from an anxiety disorder or short-term anxiety brought on by a particular stressor, such as a difficult job position or a problem in your relationship.

Cognitive behavioral therapy (CBT) may be a useful strategy to treat both anxiety and sleeplessness if they are associated (more on this later).

Additionally, you can take self-management measures for moderate anxiety by include

- Items that lower anxiety in your diet.
- Engaging in some physical activity every day
- Incorporating techniques for relaxation into your self-care regimen
- Scheduling leisure time for interests and fun activities

Insomnia Prevention

Sleep hygiene, or good sleeping habits, is a powerful tool for treating insomnia. Here are some tips:

1. Make it a habit to go to bed and wake up at the same times every day. Avoid taking naps during the day as they could cause you to feel less drowsy at night.

2. Avoid using e-books or phones right before bed. Sleeping might be more difficult because of their light.

3. Steer clear of alcohol, nicotine, and caffeine in the afternoon. Stimulants like caffeine and nicotine can prevent you from falling asleep. Alcohol can impair the quality of your sleep and cause you to wake up in the middle of the night.

4. Engage in regular exercise. Avoid working out right before bed as this could interfere with your ability to fall asleep. Exercise at least three to four hours before bed, according to experts.

5. Avoid consuming a large meal in the afternoon. But having a small snack before bed might promote better sleep.

6. Make sure your bedroom is cozy—it should be quiet, dark, and neither too hot nor too chilly. If you have trouble sleeping, wear a sleeping mask. Try using a white noise machine, a fan, or earplugs to muffle noise.

7. Follow a routine to relax before bed. Take a bath, read a book, or listen to music.
   Your bed should only be used for sleeping and having sex.

8. Get up and do something relaxing, like reading, until you feel sleepy if you are having trouble falling asleep and aren't already exhausted.

9. Make a to-do list before bed if you often find yourself lying awake worrying about things. This could assist you in putting your worries aside for the evening.

Healthy Sleeping Habits to Avoid Insomnia

1. Maintain a consistent bedtime and wake-up time every day, even on the weekends.
Stay active. A restful night's sleep might result from regular activity.

2. Take fewer naps or none at all.

3. Limit or do not use caffeine, alcohol and nicotine.

4. Avoid consuming heavy meals or a lot of liquids right before bed.

5. Make your bedroom cozy and reserve it for sleeping or having sex.

6. Establish a calming bedtime routine, such reading a book, having a warm bath, or listening to peaceful music.

While many causes of insomnia are avoidable, there are other causes that may arise for unclear reasons. Even while there is no way to completely prevent insomnia, there are many of things you can do to improve your sleep.

Living with Insomnia

How do I take care of myself?

Sleep hygiene is a key component of many of the most effective strategies you may use to treat insomnia and improve your quality of sleep in general. These consist of, but are not restricted to:

1. Assign and adhere to a sleep schedule. Having a schedule is, for the majority of people, the best thing you can do for your body and sleep demands.

2. Establish a bedtime and try your best to stick to it— even on the weekends, on holidays, on vacation, etc.

3. Avoid taking naps in the late afternoon or early evening as these can disrupt your sleep pattern.

4. Instead, try not to rely on napping.

5. Allow yourself some time to relax. Try your best to set the day's worries aside before going to bed.

6. Include a buffer period of time between your end of the day and your bedtime. You may be able to sleep better after doing that.

7. If you have trouble falling asleep, consider doing something quiet or soothing instead than lying in bed all night.

8. Make yourself comfy. Having a good night's sleep is highly dependent on your comfort level.

9. Make the appropriate adjustments to the temperature, lighting, and noise level for your sleeping space. You might want to give this a try as well.

10. Some individuals find that using a sound generator that plays a particular frequency of sound helps them fall asleep.

11. Put that device down. The light used by electronic devices usually fools your brain into believing it is not nightfall. That may interfere with the molecules that alert your body and brain when it's time to go to sleep.

12. Be mindful of what you consume. Overindulging in food or beverages, as well as staying up late, might have an impact on your sleep quality. Certain foods

and beverages, particularly those high in caffeine or alcohol content or nicotine products, might also interfere with your ability to sleep.

13. Continue to move. Even a little exercise, like walking, can improve the quality of your sleep.

14. Consult your healthcare professional if you have problems falling asleep on a regular basis.

15. You can concentrate on improving your sleep quality and understanding the reason behind your insomnia by consulting with your primary care physician.

16. Detecting any health problems that can interfere with your sleep might also be aided by them.

What are the risk factors for Insomnia?

Insomnia is also more likely to happen in people with the following characteristics or circumstances:

- Light-sleepers.
- Those who take alcohol.
- Individuals who don't feel safe in their homes (due to circumstances like abuse or violence that occurs frequently).
- Those who have sleep-related fears or anxieties, such as those who suffer from nightmare disorders or nocturnal panic attacks.

The risk of insomnia can be raised by a variety of reasons. Women have insomnia more frequently than males do, as do older persons than younger ones. African Americans who are young or middle-aged also have an increased risk.

Other risk factors include:
- Long-term illness
- Mental health problems
- Working rotating or night shifts

- Older age
- Family history of insomnia
- Certain occupations, such as shift or night work, or jobs that require travelling to different time zones
- Stress
- Being a woman
- A sedentary lifestyle
- Unpredictable sleep-wake cycles or a schedule that is frequently altered due to shift
- Employment or job hours
- Taking naps
- Drinking a lot of caffeine
- Alcohol and tobacco use
- Difficulty winding down at bedtime
- Waking up frequently to tend to a baby

Furthermore, some medications can make it difficult to fall or remain asleep. These may consist of:
Beta-blockers
Antidepressants
Decongestants
Diuretics
Medications that replace nicotine
Steroid

Though it can affect people of any age or gender, older adults right before, during, and after menopause are the most prevalent times for insomnia to manifest.

Insomnia risk factors can also include: excessive levels of stress, which can be related to problems in life, money problems, or issues with family and relationships

What are the complications of Insomnia?

Your health depends on sleep just as much as it does on a balanced diet and regular exercise. insomnia is the cause of your sleeplessness, which can have both physical and mental effects. Those who struggle with insomnia tend to report a worse quality of life than those who get enough sleep.

Sleep is necessary for our bodies and minds to heal. It's also essential for memory retention and learning. If you're having trouble sleeping, you may have: A higher risk of falling, if you're an older woman
Difficulty concentrating
Grumpiness
Slow reaction time that can lead to a car crash

Sleep deprivation results from insomnia that is severe or persistent. Daytime sleepiness is a key worry associated with sleep deprivation, and it can be harmful when driving or performing other duties requiring alertness and attentiveness.
Lack of sleep can also raise your risk of developing other conditions:
Depression.

Fear and anxiety.
Elevated blood pressure, or hypertension.
Heart attack.
Stroke.
Apnea obstructive sleep.
Type 2 diabetes.
Obesity.
Conditions that involve psychosis.

Insomnia-related complications can include:

- Poorer performance in the workplace or in school.
- Slowed reaction time while driving and a higher risk of accidents.
- Mental health conditions, such as depression, anxiety or substance misuse.
- Increased susceptibility to or exacerbation of chronic illnesses or ailments, including
- Hypertension and cardiovascular disease.

When should I see a healthcare provider?

If your insomnia starts to interfere with your everyday activities, tasks, and routine, or if it persists for more than a few nights, you should consult your healthcare practitioner (particularly a primary care physician). Also, you ought to speak with them if you observe the following:

Your significant other has noticed that you appear to briefly cease breathing at night, which is sometimes accompanied by loud snoring; this could be an indication of sleep apnea.

You have been taking medication for more than a few nights without success, or your prescription is no longer working for you to sleep.

A medical professional may classify insomnia as acute if it persists for many weeks or longer. Chronic insomnia is what's called on when it persists for three months or more. Short-term sleeplessness can cause drowsiness during the day, difficulties focusing, and other issues. Long-term, it might raise the chance of developing a number of illnesses.

If your sleeplessness interferes with your ability to perform everyday tasks, consult your physician or another primary care provider. Your physician will look for the source of your sleep issue and assist in its treatment. In the event that your doctor believes you may have a sleep disorder, they may advise visiting a sleep center for more testing.

It's difficult to fight feeling sleepy during the day. Micro sleeps are brief periods of time during the day when you are asleep, usually occurring while you are working or driving.

If you suffer from any other illnesses that limit the amount or quality of your sleep, such as mental health issues.

What questions should I ask my doctor?

Is my physical health interfering with my ability to sleep, and are there any symptoms or other conditions I should be aware of?
How are my medications (if you take any) affecting my sleep?
What can I do if I think my mental health is affecting how I sleep?

Can being pregnant affect how I sleep?
Yes, pregnancy-related problems and being pregnant itself can have a major impact on your sleep quality. Pregnancy frequently brings about changes in the physical, hormonal, and psychological aspects of the body. These may disrupt your sleep cycle and make it more difficult to obtain adequate restorative sleep. Speak with your healthcare practitioner if you're pregnant and finding it difficult to fall asleep. They can frequently assist you in better understanding the reasons behind your poor sleep quality and self-help techniques.

Symptoms of Insomnia

Some signs of insomnia could be:

- Difficulty going asleep at night.
- Waking up in the dead of night.
- Waking up earlier than usual.
- Being drowsy or exhausted during the day.
- Feeling cranky, depressed or anxious.
- Having a hard time paying attention, focusing on tasks or remembering.
- Making more errors or having more accidents.
- Worrying about sleep all the time.

In addition to causing sleep disturbances, insomnia can cause additional problems such as

Daytime tiredness or drowsiness,
Sadness, or anxiety.
Low motivation or energy
Inadequate focus and concentration, a lack of
Coordination, and hasty decisions can result in mistakes or accidents.
Worries or annoyances regarding sleep inadequate performance at work or school challenges interacting with others, working, or studying

There are various possible symptoms of insomnia that can be divided into numerous categories:

- When you have trouble sleeping.
- Daytime effects.

When you have trouble sleeping
One of the main signs of insomnia is difficulty sleeping. There are three primary methods in which this occurs, and individuals frequently alternate between them over time:
Initial insomnia (beginning of sleep): This indicates that you have difficulty sleeping.
Insomnia of the middle (maintenance) kind causes you to wake up in the middle of the night but go back to sleep. It is the most prevalent type, impacting over two-thirds of those who suffer from insomnia.
Early morning/late night insomnia: This form indicates that you wake up too early and refuse to go back to sleep.

Daytime effects
You need sleep to function at your best, thus sleep disturbances like insomnia frequently result in symptoms that you experience during the day. Among them are:
Feeling drowsy, fatigued, or sick.
Delayed reactions, like responding too slowly while

Operating a motor vehicle.
Difficulty recalling details.
Slowed thinking, perplexity, or difficulty focusing.
Disturbances in mood, including anxiety, melancholy, and impatience.
Various hiccups in your regular activities, hobbies, social life, or place of employment.

What causes Insomnia

The underlying causes of insomnia typically have a significant impact on the sort of insomnia you encounter. Numerous variables might lead to insomnia. These can differ from person to person and there might not always be a clear reason for them. On the other hand, stress, anxiety, and sadness are a few typical reasons of insomnia.

Although the exact causes of insomnia are unknown, experts currently believe that a variety of factors may be involved. Some of these elements may be contributing factors or they may even be the cause. Further investigation is required to precisely comprehend the causes and mechanisms of insomnia.

The following are some possible causes or contributing factors, but they're not the only ones:

Genetic family history: Insomnia and other sleep disorders appear to run in families.

Brain activity differences: It's possible that brain chemistry variations or increased brain activity in people with insomnia interfere with their ability to fall asleep.

Medical conditions: Your physical well-being can have an impact on how well you sleep. This covers both acute ailments like small wounds or infections and long-term ailments like Parkinson's disease or acid reflux. Other influences include circumstances that alter your circadian rhythm, or your body's internal clock for sleep and wakefulness.

Mental health issues: Approximately 50% of those with chronic insomnia also suffer from at least one additional mental illness, such as sadness or anxiety.

Life circumstances: Stressful or difficult life circumstances may not necessarily cause insomnia, but it's very common for them to contribute to it.

Life changes: Short-term or transient changes, such as jet lag, sleeping somewhere new, or getting used to a new work schedule (particularly shift work), are frequently contributing factors. Sleep can also be impacted by long-term changes, such as moving to a new house.

Your daily routine and habits: Sleep hygiene, or your sleeping patterns, may be a factor in your insomnia. This covers your sleeping schedule, whether or not you take naps, when you drink coffee, and other routines.

Chronic insomnia is typically brought on by stress, occurrences in life, or sleep-depriving behaviors. Even though treating the underlying cause of your insomnia may make it go away, insomnia can occasionally persist for years.

Common causes of long-term insomnia

Stress. It can be difficult to fall asleep at night when your mind is racing with worries about your family, career, education, health, or finances. Insomnia can also result from stressful life events like divorce, losing one's job, or a loved one passing away or becoming unwell.

Work or travel schedule. Circadian rhythms, also referred to as your body's "internal clock," regulate bodily temperature, metabolism, and sleep-wake cycles. Sleep disturbances can result in insomnia. Experiencing jet lag due to frequent shift changes, working late or early hours, or traveling across many time zones are among the causes.

Poor sleep habits. Having an uncomfortable sleeping space, napping, being overly active before bed, and having various wake-up and bedtimes are all examples of poor sleep hygiene. Other sleep-depriving behaviors include eating, working, or watching TV in bed. Your sleep cycle might be disturbed by using cellphones or laptops right before bed, playing video games, or watching TV.

Eating too much late in the evening. It's okay to have a small snack before going to bed. However, eating too much could make it difficult for you to lie down comfortably. Heartburn is another common ailment. This occurs when the tube that transports food from your mouth to your stomach becomes clogged with stomach acid. The esophagus is the name of this tube. You might not sleep through heartburn.

Mental health disorders. Sleep disturbances can be caused by anxiety disorders, including post-traumatic stress disorder. An indication of depression may be waking up too early. Many times, insomnia coexists with other mental health issues.

Medicines. Numerous prescription medications, including some antidepressants and those for blood pressure or asthma, can cause sleep disturbances. Numerous over-the-counter medications, including some pain relievers, cold and allergy remedies, and weight-loss drugs, contain stimulants like caffeine that can interfere with sleep.

Medical conditions. Chronic pain, diabetes, heart illness, asthma, GERD (gastric reflux disease), an overactive thyroid, Parkinson's disease, Alzheimer's disease, and asthma are a few diseases that have been related to sleeplessness.

Sleep-related disorders. Breathing stops intermittently during the night due to sleep apnea, which interferes with your sleep. When you're attempting to fall asleep, restless legs syndrome gives you a strong, uncomfortable need to move your legs. This can prevent you from drifting off to sleep or from waking up again.

Alcohol, nicotine, and caffeine. Stimulants include coffee, tea, cola, and other beverages containing caffeine. If you consume them in the late afternoon or evening, you may avoid dozing off at night. Tobacco products contain nicotine, another stimulant that can interfere with sleep. While alcohol may aid in falling asleep, it also keeps you from reaching deeper sleep stages and frequently causes you to wake up in the middle of the night.

Common causes of insomnia

Insomnia can be caused by stress or mental health problems in certain individuals. Someone could be going through:
Depression
Bipolar disorder anxiety
Schizophrenia

Other medical disorders that may interfere with sleep

Restless legs syndrome.
An overactive thyroid
Sleep apnea
Gastrointestinal reflux disease (GERD)
Chronic obstructive pulmonary disease (COPD)
Chronic pain
Alzheimer's disease

Rarely, some people may inherit a fatal family insomnia condition. This hereditary disorder may result in brain damage and insomnia, both of which can be fatal.

The most typical reasons why people have insomnia

Depression

Anxiety

Stress

Sounds

A very hot or cold room

Uncomfortable mattresses

Illicit substances like cocaine or ecstasy alcohol, coffee, or nicotine

Jet lag

Shift work

Can COVID-19 cause insomnia?

Yes, COVID-19 can interfere with your sleep, although the exact mechanism and cause of this are still unknown to scientists. The precise ways in which COVID-19 impacts your body and mind are being studied by researchers. They also believe that this could be partially explained by the general stress brought on by the COVID-19 pandemic.

If you have acute insomnia, for example, these could be the causes:
Stress an unpleasant or traumatic occurrence modifications to your sleeping patterns, such as your first

experience sleeping in a new house, hotel, or with a
partner physical discomfort or sickness
jet lag and specific drugs

Chronic pain issues like back pain or arthritis can
cause chronic insomnia, or it can happen on its own.
psychological problems such substance abuse disorders,
anxiety, or sadness
Various sleep disorders, including sleep apnea
health conditions such as diabetes, cancer, gastro
esophageal reflux disease (GERD), or cardiovascular
disease

STAGES AND TYPES OF INSOMNIA

At some point, many adults have short-term insomnia. Days or weeks may pass during this. Stress or a traumatic experience is typically the cause of short-term sleeplessness. However, some people develop chronic insomnia, also known as long-term insomnia. This continues for at least three months. The primary issue could be insomnia, or it could be connected to other illnesses or medications.

Doctors may also classify it by cause. For example, primary insomnia is an issue by itself and secondary insomnia is a result of another health issue. They might also employ instruments like the insomnia severity index and categorize it according to severity.

Experts generally classify insomnia into two primary categories:

Experts classify insomnia as acute (short-term) or chronic (long-term). We refer to the chronic form as insomnia disorder.

There are two types of insomnia: primary and secondary.

Primary insomnia: This indicates that there is no connection between your sleep issues and any other illness or issue.

Secondary insomnia: This refers to difficulty falling asleep as a result of a medical condition (such as depression, cancer, arthritis, heartburn, or asthma); pain; medication; or drug abuse (such as alcohol).

Various descriptions of insomnia are offered by experts, based on the particular features of the condition:

Short-term sleeping problems that often don't last longer than a few weeks are referred to as acute insomnia.

When you experience insomnia for three or more days per week on a regular basis, usually for three months or more, it's referred to as chronic insomnia.

The term "onset insomnia" refers to trouble falling asleep. In addition to being caused by traditional insomnia triggers like caffeine usage, mental health issues, or other environmental factors, difficulty falling

asleep can also arise from other sleep disorders.
When you regularly wake up too early or have difficulty staying asleep once you fall asleep, you are said to have maintenance insomnia. Lying awake at night worried that you won't get enough sleep can exacerbate insomnia of this kind, which may be related to underlying medical conditions and mental health issues.

Childhood behavioral insomnia is characterized by persistent difficulty falling asleep, refusal to go to bed, or both. Following a regular sleep schedule and adopting self-soothing techniques are generally beneficial for children with this disease.

Additionally, insomnia may be secondary (comorbid) or primary (idiopathic).
There is no known cause or underlying medical or mental health issue with primary insomnia. In contrast, secondary insomnia is associated with underlying reasons such as persistent pain or sickness.
mental health issues such as anxiety or sadness
shift job with specific drugs

In the past, certain rules might have distinguished between different types of insomnia. These include:

- Psychophysiological
- Insomnia idiopathic

- Insomnia paradoxical insomnia
- Inadequate sleep hygiene
- Behavioral insomnia of childhood
- Insomnia due to a mental health condition
- Insomnia due to medical condition
- Insomnia due to a drug or substance

Characteristics of chronic insomnia

It's also critical to consider the features of insomnia symptoms. You might have persistent insomnia if certain symptoms apply to you. Among the traits are:

Circumstances: For an insomnia diagnosis to be considered chronic, there must be no sleep-inducing circumstances (e.g., work schedule changes, life events, etc.). Having trouble falling asleep even when you have the time and space to do so is necessary for diagnosing insomnia.

Frequency: Having insomnia frequently—at least three times a week—is necessary for chronic insomnia. Duration: Chronic insomnia lasts for at least three months.

Explanation: Substances, pharmaceuticals (including prescription and over-the-counter), or other sleep disorders are not the cause of the insomnia. Your inability to fall asleep is also not entirely explained by other physical or mental health issues.

Management and Treatment

The two major methods for treating insomnia are:

1. creating and adhering to healthy sleeping practices, or "sleep hygiene."
2. Drugs that aid in falling or staying asleep, particularly those that don't create habits or have the potential to interfere with your sleep otherwise.

Mental healthcare

Mental healthcare is one of the best ways to enhance your sleep, either directly or indirectly, since it has a significant impact on your capacity to fall asleep. The greatest person to enlighten you about your alternatives for mental health treatment and to give you information on where to find this type of care is a healthcare professional.

Medications that help you fall or stay asleep

Medication comes in a wide variety that can aid in falling or staying asleep. Medications for mental health, specific herbs and vitamins, and prescription and over-the-counter sedatives and hypnotics make up a large number of these. Sedative drugs: The Latin term that means "to settle" is where these receive their name. They lessen the activity of the neurological system.

Hypnotic drugs: These get their name from Hypnos, the Greek god of sleep. These induce drowsiness. Generally speaking, the best person to inform you about potential therapies and which ones they recommend for you is your healthcare professional. They are also the greatest source of knowledge regarding any potential adverse effects or treatment-related problems. prescription medications for sleep disorders

The following information contains examples of medications, but it isn't a list of every treatment available. Keep in mind that not everyone responds well to drugs intended to treat insomnia. Your age and physical condition can play a part, and certain medications can mix with other prescriptions. It's also critical to remember that although certain medications can improve your sleep, others may have the opposite effect on your sleep pattern. It's crucial to get quality sleep as well as quantity. This implies that you should use all medications, even over-the-counter ones, with caution.

Insomnia can be treated with a variety of pharmaceutical medications. Certain pharmaceuticals may be subject to legal restrictions based on their effects or mode of operation, depending on your location.

Controlled drug type

Dual orexin receptor antagonists (DORAs): In your brain, orexin is a neurotransmitter that promotes wakefulness. Sleeping is aided by blocking orexin. Suvorexant (Belsomra®), lemborexant (Dayvigo®), and daridorexant (Quviviq®) are a few examples of these.

Antiseizure medications: These include gabapentin (Neurontin®) and pregabalin(Lyrica®), which can help with conditions like restless leg syndrome, which can keep you awake.

Noncontrolled drug types

Sedating antidepressants: These include tricyclic antidepressant (TCA) drugs like doxepin (Silenor®) and amitriptyline(Elavil®), and trazodone.

Melatonin and related drugs: Your brain uses the hormone melatonin to signal when it's time to go to sleep. Lower strengths are available over-the-counter*, and it is also available in prescription strength. Additionally, some synthetic medications, such as ramelteon (Rozerem®), function similarly to melatonin.

Nonprescription drugs for insomnia

Drugs used to treat allergies called antihistamines can also put you to sleep. Examples of this include diphenhydramine (the active ingredient in drugs like Benadryl®) and doxylamine (commonly known under the brand name Unisom®).

Herbs and supplements

Many herbs or supplements can help treat insomnia. Even if a lot of these are well-known and widely used, it's wise to avoid assuming that a herb or supplement is safe for you just because it is. Before using herbs and supplements, consult a healthcare professional. This aids in preventing any negative effects or interactions, particularly if you take any other medications or have any medical issues.

Diagnosing insomnia

A sleep expert can assist with the diagnosis and management of sleep issues. They might:

Ask the person about their medical history, sleep patterns, and use of drugs and alcohol
perform a physical assessment to look for any underlying issues.

Request an overnight sleep test to record sleep patterns suggest wearing a device that tracks movement and sleep-wake patterns

The Diagnostic and Statistical Manual of Mental Disorders, Fifth Edition (DSM-V) states that if any of the following conditions are satisfied, a physician may diagnose insomnia:

- Dissatisfaction with sleep quality or quantity
- Considerable distress with one's ability to operate in
- Daily life as a result of sleep difficulties
- The sleep difficulty occurs at least 3 times a week
- The sleep difficulty is present for at least 3 months
- The sleep difficulty occurs despite adequate
- Opportunity and circumstances for sleep

A complaint of one or more of the following sleep difficulties:

- Difficulty initiating sleep
- Difficulty maintaining sleep
- Early morning awakening no restorative sleep

How is insomnia diagnosed?

A medical professional may use a variety of techniques to diagnose insomnia, including questioning you about your symptoms, sleep patterns, personal circumstances, and medical history. In order to rule out other illnesses that might contribute to or cause insomnia, they might also suggest certain testing.

What tests will be done to diagnose insomnia?

There are no diagnostic tests specifically designed to identify insomnia. Rather than that, testing assist in ruling out other illnesses that share symptoms with insomnia. The most likely tests include:

- Sleep apnea testing involving an overnight sleep study in a sleep lab (polysomnography) or an at-home sleep apnea screening device.
- Actorexia.
- Multiple sleep latency test (MSLT).

Getting a diagnosis

Along with a physical examination, your doctor will inquire about your medical and sleep history.

They could advise you to record your sleep patterns and day-to-day feelings in a sleep diary for a week or two. They might discuss how much and how well you're sleeping with your bed companion. Sleep centers may also require you to undergo certain testing.

A medical expert will typically inquire about the following when contemplating an insomnia diagnosis:
any current medical conditions
physical and mental health symptoms you've noticed stressors in your personal or professional life sleep history, including how long you've had insomnia symptoms and how they affect your daily life

They can utilize this information to identify the root reasons of your sleep issues. They may also ask you to keep a sleep log for 2 to 4 weeks, tracking:
- What time you go to bed
- The approximate time it takes you to fall asleep
- Any instances of repeated waking in the night
- What time you wake up each day

A written or app-based sleep log will give your healthcare team a clearer picture of your sleep patterns. In order to help rule out medical disorders that could interfere with your sleep, they can also conduct blood work or medical testing. They might advise taking part in a sleep study if they think you might have an underlying sleep issue, such as obstructive sleep apnea.

What does a sleep study involve?

Participation in a sleep study can be done in one of two ways:

An overnight stay at a sleep center

At home, in your own bed

Electrodes are applied to various parts of your body, including your head, in both sleep study choices. In order to classify your sleep states and track your movements while you're asleep, the electrodes record your brain waves.

Your doctor will receive valuable neuroelectrical and physiological data from your sleep study that will help them make a more accurate diagnosis of sleep disorders. A clinical diagnosis of insomnia is likely to be given to you if you have both of the following symptoms:

sleep difficulties occurring at least 3 nights a week for a minimum of 3 months

sleep difficulties creating major distress or difficulties in daily life

MYTHS ABOUT INSOMNIA

Myth 1: Having insomnia means you frequently struggle to fall asleep

Fact: You may have insomnia if you have difficulty falling or staying asleep, including waking up before your alarm.

Having problems sleeping or staying asleep, or experiencing poor quality sleep, is known as insomnia. Your physician might be able to diagnose you with acute insomnia if you have these sleep problems at least three evenings a week (Trusted Source). You might have chronic insomnia if you have sleeplessness three evenings a week or more for a duration of three months.

Myth 2: You can catch up on lost sleep

Fact: Sleeping later on weekends won't make up for the sleep you missed during the week.

You accrue sleep debt if you regularly miss sleep each night. This represents the overall quantity of sleep lost over time.

Sleeping in on the weekends may make you feel better, but it can also make insomnia worse. Your sleep-wake cycle may be disturbed if you oversleep on some days.

Myth 3: There is no remedy for insomnia

Fact: There are numerous approaches to managing and treating insomnia.

There are actions you can do at home to control your sleeplessness. You might also discuss cognitive behavioral therapy or medication with a physician or sleep specialist if you suffer from chronic insomnia. Treating any underlying medical disorders, such as anxiety or sleep apnea, that may be causing your sleeplessness, may also help.

Myth 4: All sleep aids are created equal.

Fact: The methods by which different classes of insomnia drugs aid in sleep are distinct.

Medication alternatives for insomnia are numerous. While some aid in getting you to sleep, others aid in keeping you sleeping. Some people combine the two.

Myth 5: You ought to remain in bed until you sleep off.

Fact: Lying in bed awake can increase anxious feelings about sleep.

Additionally, it may exacerbate sleeplessness by teaching your brain to link those unfavorable emotions with the bedroom.

Try to keep your bedroom solely for sleeping and having sex. Your brain may start to equate your bed with your work if your bedroom is used as an office. It could be more difficult to switch off work-related thoughts when you want to sleep.

Myth 6: Good sleep is about the number of hours
Fact: Sleep quality is also important for your health. Adults should aim for at least seven hours of sleep per night, according to a reliable source. You might not feel rested when you wake up, though.

Myth 7: Drinking alcohol improves sleep quality
Fact: Drinking alcohol in the evenings can negatively affect your sleep quality.
Alcohol use before bed may induce sleepiness.Reliable Source, yet it only puts you to sleep briefly. It's possible that you won't sleep as well at night and that you'll wake up more frequently.

Myth 8: A mental health issue is what causes insomnia
Fact: Various health conditions and behaviors can also cause insomnia.
While anxiety and post-traumatic stress disorder are two mental health problems that can cause insomnia, other medical conditions and drugs can also cause it.

Treating insomnia

The best approach can depend on the underlying cause
and the type of insomnia, but some options
Cognitive behavioral therapy (CBT)
Prescription medications
Over-the-counter sleep aids

Melatonin
But there isn't enough solid evidence to support the claim
that melatonin promotes better sleep.

Treating acute insomnia might not be necessary.
If your fatigue prevents you from performing daily tasks,
your doctor might recommend sleeping drugs for a brief
period of time. Drugs that take effect rapidly but wear off
soon can help you prevent issues like sleepiness the next
day.
For insomnia, avoid using over-the-counter sleeping
medications. They tend to operate less effectively over
time and may have negative effects.

You will require treatment for the illnesses or health
issues preventing you from sleeping if you have chronic
insomnia. Additionally, your physician may recommend
behavioral therapy. This can assist you in learning how to

encourage sleep and changing the things you do that exacerbate insomnia.

You can manage insomnia using targeted approaches that you can learn with the help of an online or in-person therapist, such as:

Stimulus control. This method reduces the amount of time you spend laying awake worried about falling asleep by teaching you to get out of bed and engage in a peaceful, soothing activity until you feel tired.

Sleep restriction. This method can help boost the quantity and quality of your sleep by initially limiting the amount of time you spend in bed and then gradually increasing it.

Bright light therapy. This method entails being in bright light either in the morning or the evening, based on whether you have more difficulty remaining asleep or falling asleep.

Along with advice on sleep hygiene practices that assist you in addressing behaviors that keep you from obtaining enough good sleep, your therapist may also provide you with information on relaxing techniques.

They might, for example, recommend you avoid:
- Drinking caffeinated beverages near bedtime
- Eating large or heavy meals or spicy foods close to bedtime
- Getting intense exercise near bedtime
- Using your bed for anything other than sleep or sex

A therapist can also assist in determining whether underlying mental health issues are aggravating your insomnia symptoms or causing them to worsen. Resolving these causes and triggers can significantly aid in the relief of sleeplessness.

Drugs and dietary supplements

Your clinician might also prescribe medication to treat insomnia, such as:
- Triazolam (Halcion),
- Zolpidem (Ambien),
- Eszopiclone (Lunesta)

Supplements like melatonin and over-the-counter (OTC) sleep aids can also provide some help from insomnia.

It is believed that taking melatonin supplements may somewhat shorten the time it takes you to fall asleep because your body naturally creates the hormone melatonin during the sleep cycle.

That However, there is still conflicting evidence to support the use of melatonin to treat insomnia. Furthermore, although melatonin is usually regarded as safe for short-term usage, doctors have not yet confirmed if it is safe to take over an extended period of time. Check in with a healthcare professional before trying supplements like melatonin or OTC medications to help ease insomnia. These drugs may have negative effects or interact with other prescription and over-the-counter drugs.

Consult your healthcare provider before taking any vitamins or drugs if you are pregnant.
Other approaches

Insomnia symptoms can frequently be controlled with a change in lifestyle and natural therapies.
Ideas to try include:
Natural sleep aids. For example, you could try valerian, warm milk, and herbal tea before bed. Fragrances that are calming, like lavender, might also have some advantages.
Meditation. This method facilitates relaxation and present-moment awareness. It does more than only facilitate falling asleep and enhance the quality of sleep.

Applications. You can start meditating with the aid of many Additionally, it can aid in the relief of pain, tension, and anxiety—all of which may contribute to sleeplessness.

Acupuncture. This is a traditional Chinese medicine practice that is useful for relieving insomnia symptoms for many people. It includes inserting small needles at pressure points throughout the body.

Home care strategies to treat Insomnia

A variety of treatments and advice can be used to treat insomnia personally at home. They entail adjustments to:

Sleeping habits

Establishing a schedule by going to bed and waking up at the same times can be helpful when feasible.
Any device with a screen should not be used immediately before bed.

An hour before going to bed, for instance, start relaxing with a bath.

Devices such as phones should not be used in bedrooms. Before going to bed, make sure the room is at a comfortable temperature.

Use drapes or blackout shades to make the space darker.

Nutritional practices

Steer clear of eating right before bed. If needed, have a nutritious snack before going to bed.
But try not to have a large dinner two or three hours before bed.

Drink less alcohol and caffeine, especially at night.
Eat a balanced, wholesome diet to improve your general wellbeing.

Peace of mind and leisure
Exercise on a regular basis, but avoid doing so right before bed.

Practice deep breathing and relaxation, particularly right before bed.

Seek out a sleeping aid, such a book or some calming music.

Even if you're tired during the day, try not to nap.
Seek medical assistance for any mental health conditions, including anxiety.

DOS AND DONT'S for self-treating insomnia

Changing your sleeping habits typically helps with insomnia.

DOS

go to bed and wake up at the same time every day
relax at least 1 hour before bed, for example, take a bath or read a book
Ensure that your bedroom is silent and dark. use curtains, blinds, an eye mask or ear plugs if needed
exercise regularly during the day make sure your mattress, pillows and covers are comfortable

DONTS

do not smoke or drink alcohol, tea or coffee at least 6 hours before going to bed do not eat a big meal late at nights
Avoid exercising at least four hours before bed.
Avoid using electronics like smartphones or televisions just
before bed because the blue light from them keeps you awake.

do not nap during the day do not drive when you feel sleepy
do not sleep in after a bad night's sleep and stick to your regular sleeping hours instead

GP treatment for insomnia

To ensure you receive the best care, your doctor will look into the cause of your sleeplessness.

You may occasionally receive an offer for cognitive behavioral treatment (CBT). This could be done online through a self-help program or in-person with a therapist. This can assist you in altering the ideas and actions that prevent you from falling asleep.

If you exhibit signs of another sleep issue, like sleep apnea, you might be referred to a sleep clinic.

Today, doctors seldom ever recommend sleeping medications to treat insomnia. In addition to their potentially dangerous negative effects, sleeping medications can cause dependence.

Only in the following situations are sleeping drugs prescribed: severe insomnia for which no other treatments have been successful; or a few days or weeks at most

Cognitive behavioral therapy for insomnia (CBT-I)

CBT-I is a type of therapy designed to teach you how to improve your quality of sleep. The method involves working with a licensed therapist for several weeks. Aspects of CBT-I often include the following: developing positive attitudes toward sleep;
Aspects of CBT-I often include:

- learning to have positive feelings about sleep
- learning that staying in bed and not sleeping can worsen insomnia
- Reducing nervousness about sleep
- Learning good sleep habits
- Practicing relaxation therapy
- Learning to maintain a regular sleep-wake cycle
- Focusing on specific periods of quality sleep (sleep restriction)

For insomnia, CBT-I is frequently the first line of treatment. A meta-analysis for 2021According to Trusted Source, CBT-I functions by modifying an individual's ideas on sleep, at least partially.

When prescribing a medication, doctors consider a number of factors, such as your age and gender, safety, potential adverse effects, combinations with other medications, and duration of usage. The qualities of the drugs, such as how soon and how long they function, are also taken into account.

Food and Drug Administration (FDA)

Approved prescription medications for insomnia in current use include:

Benzodiazepines: These are medications that promote calm, relaxation, and reduced anxiety. You may find it simpler to fall asleep as a result. Benzodiazepines are usually only recommended for brief periods of time.

Z-drugs: These pharmaceuticals function similarly to benzodiazepines. Their action slows down brain activity, which causes drowsiness. The FDATrusted Source states that those who engage in sophisticated sleep behaviors, such as sleepwalking, shouldn't use them. Complicated sleep behaviors may result from the drugs.

Melatonin receptor agonists: Prescription drugs like tasimelteon and ramelteon alter the chemicals in the brain that control the cycle of sleep and wakefulness. They assist in resetting your body's clock. Even while melatonin is also taken by many people as a sleep aid, it is not FDA-regulated and is instead regarded as a dietary supplement.

Orexin receptor antagonists: These drugs inhibit the brain chemical orexin, which promotes sleep.

Antidepressants: An extremely low dosage of doxepin has been recommended to treat sleeplessness. Antidepressants are occasionally used by doctors to treat depression and insomnia.

Another option to think about is an over-the-counter **(OTC) sleep aid**. A lot of these are drowsy-inducing antihistamines. Restless legs syndrome or restlessness can be brought on by some antihistamines.

It is important to see a physician before using any over-the-counter sleep aids or supplements.

CONCLUSION

A typical issue is insomnia. Numerous problems, some of which may be related to mental or physical health, might cause it. Sometimes they have to do with lifestyle choices or the surroundings, such working shifts or consuming alcohol or caffeine.

A lack of sleep can cause a wide range of issues, from chronic sickness to just plain weariness.

A physician should be seen if they have persistent problems falling asleep and believe that it is interfering with their daily activities. A physician can assist in determining the cause and provide a remedy.

A SLEEP DIARY

	Date	Bedtime	Total Sleep Time	Wake-Up Time	Number of Awakenings	Duration of Awakenings	Notes (e.g., stress, diet, exercise)
	[MM/DD/YYYY]	[HH]	[HH]	[Hours	[Number]	[Hours]	[Detail]
1							
2							
3							
4							
5 6							
7							

NOTES

NOTES

NOTES

NOTES

www.ingramcontent.com/pod-product-compliance
Lightning Source LLC
Chambersburg PA
CBHW031321250726
48656CB00005B/1916